Struck Down but Not Destroyed

TOM KINGERY

WESTBOW
PRESS®
A DIVISION OF THOMAS NELSON
& ZONDERVAN

WestBow Press books may be ordered through booksellers or by contacting:

WestBow Press
A Division of Thomas Nelson & Zondervan
1663 Liberty Drive
Bloomington, IN 47403
www.westbowpress.com
844-714-3454

ISBN: 978-1-6642-7898-1 (sc)
ISBN: 978-1-6642-7899-8 (e)

Library of Congress Control Number: 2022917755

Print information available on the last page.

WestBow Press rev. date: 10/18/2022

Dedicated to

JEFF,
THE SHADOW WARRIOR

CONTENTS

PREFACE

Being a pastor is hard! One thing that can be guaranteed in the ministry is that it will be a mixed blessing. All any of us humans can ever know in their life's journey is a mixed blessing. Life for the "called," however, can be quite bittersweet. The glory of the good news is often met by the woes of the world. There is indifference and disdain. There is ignorance and apathy, disinterest and lukewarmness, heedlessness and disregard.

At the same time, we can be met with a joyful eagerness. Many of the people we serve will gladly hear the gospel of Christ. There can be enthusiasm and wonder, readiness and desire, and love and devotion! Many come truly seeking the "shot in the arm" a good sermon can give. Many express appreciation for the spirit we bring into their midst—a spirit of righteousness and truth, of faith and sincerity, of honesty and integrity. Some people will clean up their act when we enter the scene, while some will just not care or walk away.

Perhaps in this book, I am writing about the impossibility of our task. We are to bring the enlightenment of Christ into a world that seems so full of darkness. We are to orchestrate the conversion of the souls of men and women who often would rather not have to change. We have all the best answers, but too few are asking questions. We hope to excite people with the knowledge that excites us. We want to teach something good to people who think they already know everything. I know, for example, a wonderful environmentalist who sees the obvious dangers of continuing in our current world with business as usual concerning the impending disasters of climate change and who struggles with his efforts to change the ways people think. Everyone who seeks to nurture the visionary possibilities by which the world needs to be convinced often will feel as though they are going against the tide. But we who have the vision, can feel the tide changing. A new and brighter day is on the horizon.

Let us have the calm and visionary resolve of the one who penned the Twenty-Third Psalm:

The Lord is my shepherd, I shall not want.
He makes me lie down in green pastures;
he leads me beside still waters,
he restores my soul.
He leads me in right paths for his name's sake.
Even though I walk through the darkest valley,
I fear no evil; for you are with me;
your rod and your staff—they comfort me.
You prepare a table before me in the presence of my enemies;
you anoint my head with oil;
my cup overflows.
Surely goodness and mercy shall follow me all the days of my life,
and I shall dwell in the house of the Lord my whole life long.

With this psalm in mind, I was drawn to 2 Corinthians 4:8–10, which inspired me as if these lines themselves formed a poem:

We are afflicted in every way,
but not crushed;
perplexed,
but not driven to despair;
persecuted,
but not forsaken;
struck down,
but not destroyed;
always carrying in the body the death of Jesus,
so that the life of Jesus may also be manifested in our bodies.

INTRODUCTION

There is a wonderful "we" in Paul's second letter to the Corinthians. As the author, Paul gets very autobiographical as he deals with people in the "complaints department" of the congregation. He defends himself as a pastor, as a preacher, and as an apostle. He is compelled to counter the claims of those he calls "super-apostles" (2 Coriunthians 11:5). And he commends himself to the better judgment of those in the leadership of the church at Corinth.

Paul was the first to bring the good news of Jesus Christ to the people at this burgeoning seaport. He was not alone, but he was the leader among these witnesses to the Faith. However it happened, eventually there were some people in the congregation at Corinth who thought negatively about Paul. It seems they thought they could do a better job than he was doing. And in some respects, they tried to undermine his work, deflate his authority, and elevate themselves in his absence.

I can almost picture Paul with his fellow servants meeting to commiserate concerning the complaints against them and, especially, against himself. They are trying to see the positive truth through it all, and they come up with the list of woes and blessings recorded in 2 Corinthians 4:8–10. They have been afflicted, perplexed, persecuted, and struck down. But by the grace of God, they have not been crushed, driven to despair, forsaken, or destroyed. There is a positivity upholding them in their ministry. Every servant in every field needs to hear those positive notes when the discordant sounds become so loud. We all need to remember that though we may be mere jars of clay, there is a treasure in our lives and upon our hearts that makes us able to bear up under the difficulties of ministry. There is more reason to rejoice in our faith than to grieve our shortcomings. God is with us through it all!

This book is a series of reflections on the challenges of our ministries, the attitudes that often confront pastors and those in the service of the Church and the world, and the power of Christ that upholds us all. Each chapter will feature a short reflection on Psalm 23, relevant passages of scripture to inspire a deeper understanding of the overall challenges of ministry, a pastoral to-do list, a prayer, and an original poem or song.

SCRIPTURES

The Lord is my light and my salvation; whom shall I fear? The Lord is the stronghold of my life; of whom shall I fear? (Psalm 27:1)

Be strong, and let your heart take courage, all you who wait for the Lord. (Psalm 31:24)

"Make the mind of this people dull, and stop their ears, and shut their eyes, so that they may not look with their eyes, and listen with their ears, and comprehend with their minds, and turn and be healed." (Isaiah 6:10)

He gives power to the faint and strengthens the powerless. (Isaiah 40:29)

He has said, "I will never leave you or forsake you." So we can say with confidence, "The Lord is my helper; I will not be afraid. What can anyone do to me?" (Hebrews 13:5b–6)

My brothers and sisters, whenever you face various trials of any kind, consider it nothing but joy, because you know that the testing of your faith produces endurance; and let endurance have its effect, so that you may be mature and complete, lacking in nothing. (James 1:2–4)

In this you rejoice, even if now for a little while you have had to suffer various trials, so that the genuineness of your faith—being more precious than gold that, though perishable, is tested by fire – may be found to result in praise and glory and honor when Jesus Christ is revealed. (1 Peter 1:6–7)

Beloved, do not be surprised at the fiery ordeal that is taking place among you to test you, as though something strange were happening to you. But rejoice insomuch as you are sharing Christ's sufferings, so that you may also be glad and shout for joy when his glory is revealed. (1 Peter 4:12–13)

The one who is in you is greater than the one who is in the world. (1 John 4:4)

There is no fear in love, but perfect love casts out fear; for fear has to do with punishment, and whoever fears has not reached perfection in love. (1 John 4:18)

I lift up my eyes to the hills – from where does my help come? My help comes from the Lord, who made heaven and earth. He will not let your foot be moved; he who keeps you will not stumble. He whom keeps Israel will neither slumber nor sleep. The Lord is your keeper; the Lord is your shade at your right hand. The sun shall not strike you by day, nor the moon by night. The Lord will keep you from all evil; he will keep your life. The Lord will keep your going out and your coming in from this time on and forevermore. (Psalm 121)

What to Do

Every chapter will feature a to-do list to help you focus and take action. But to get started, here are some to-do items for the congregation that we as pastors might wish for.

- Honor those who bring the good news of the gospel.
- Add fuel to your pastor's fire—don't pour cold water on it.
- Be an encourager and a supporter of the pastor.
- Realize the "impossibility" of the preacher's task.
- Appreciate your pastor for the messages they bring and for the service they give.
- October is Clergy Appreciation Month. Rally your congregation to that purpose.
- Don't complain … too loud.

- When things are going well for the church, give the pastor some credit.
- Admittedly, pastors can be foolish at times, misguided at others. Be the one who helps rather than one who just finds fault.
- There are no prizes for finding fault. Find solutions!
- Realize that the worst time to offer criticism to a pastor is just before worship.

PRAYER

O Lord, give me grace to hold my candle high in the darkness of this world. Help me to do all that I can to cut through the shadows of doubt and ignorance, of indifference and lethargy; and keep me focused on the light I am able to see rather than the absence of light I know exists. Help my light to shine; help my fire burn; and help my knowledge of the truth give direction to those who need it. I ask this prayer in Jesus's name. Amen.

POEM
Beyond This Endless Sea

I sway upon an endless sea
And dream about a home for me—
A shoreline that is washed by peace
With tender waves that never cease
To keep their rhythm with the sand
That's changeless where my heart would stand.

Instead my heart is on a raft;
It's left swaying fore and aft.
An endless hope, an endless sea:
The two meet at infinity.
And swelling, dreaming towards that shore,
I reach where hearts have touched before.

But the timeless waves on which I sway
Just keep that home so far away.

CHAPTER 1

We Have This Ministry

Since it is by God's mercy that we are engaged in this ministry, we do not lose heart. We have renounced the shameful things that one hides, we refuse to practice cunning or to falsify God's word; but by the open statement of the truth we commend ourselves to the conscience of everyone in the sight of God. And even if our gospel is veiled, it is veiled to those who are perishing. In their case the god of this world has blinded the minds of the unbelievers, to keep them from seeing the light of the glory of Christ, who is the image of God. For we do not proclaim ourselves, we proclaim Jesus Christ as Lord and ourselves as your slaves for Jesus' sake. For it is the God who said, "Let light shine out of darkness," who has shone in our hearts to give the light of the knowledge of the glory of God in the face of Jesus Christ. (2 Corinthians 4:1–6)

We have integrity. In the New International Version, 2 Corinthians 4:1 says, "it is through God's mercy that we have *this ministry*" (emphasis mine). The NIV translation is the inspiration for the title of this chapter.

Paul's words are very affirming. What we have is not just a role to play but a validated purpose, an endowment. A diploma can affirm that we have gained a certain degree of knowledge. We are given a title, a status, a commission. We are *engaged* in what we know. Our ministry, our work, our teaching, and our leadership are things for which we are qualified. "We have this ministry!"

And because we have this ministry, "we do not lose heart" (2 Corinthians 4:1b). The reason: "God … has shone in our hearts to give the light of the knowledge of the glory of God" (2 Corinthians 4:6). We have been given light. In that light there is knowledge, and in that knowledge is the glory of God. There is integrity! We might lose heart when we forget this or take it for granted. But it must be nurtured, and it must be remembered. It must be practiced. We need to return to the experiences we have had that brought us enlightenment and inspiration. Sometimes, we need to look at the diploma or the certificate that acknowledges it.

We don't necessarily have integrity just because we have left behind "shameful things" (v. 2a) or the "practice of cunning" (v. 2b) or the "falsifying of God's word" (v. 2c). But because of this and "the open statement of the truth" (v. 2d), we can "commend ourselves to everyone's conscience" (v. 2e). We are righteous, not shameful; sincere, not cunning; honest, not false. We are true to our purpose.

So what *is* this ministry that *we* have? Well, first of all, we're not unlike Paul. He was met with resistance almost everywhere he went. What he proclaimed seemed like something mythical to many Gentiles. A resurrection? A crucified Savior? Love rather than a nationalistic focus? Grace rather than law? Many of the things he preached were contrary to the current ways or philosophies of the world. At the same time, his message was welcomed, people were inspired, and the gatherings in the name of Christ grew and were sustained.

We may be involved with the professional ministry, teaching, nursing, policing, or even politics, but we have all felt, if not actually said, "This is not what I signed up for!" We have all had to do some things for which we were not trained. Cleaning up is one of them. We may do it because it is needed. For example, cops and other first responders have to peel injured bodies out of mangled cars; teachers have to discipline students for disruptive behavior; nurses have to comfort a family when their loved one has passed away. Pastors are often asked to do secretarial work. None of these things is wrong or worthless. But when we went into our respective fields, we wanted more than anything to be protectors, light bearers, nurturers, innovators, and inspirers. Often our activities are very gratifying, and that keeps us going. But in the midst of it all, there is that mixed blessing. We may feel as though we have failed or neglected something. Compliments are encouraging, but complaints become like a dull ache that doesn't go away easily. And then we dwell on them. Problems arise even in the midst of effective accomplishments. Burnout sneaks in. We get tired, lose focus, and feel doubt.

In the ministry, and probably in other fields of service like those I've named (and how many others have not I named?), personal doubt can lead to broader doubts about the faith to which we are called. Even a "calling" can come into question.

Paul may have thought of all his wonderful qualifications when his leadership was challenged. He spent several verses in 2 Corinthians 11 boasting. He agrees that it is foolish to do so, but he enumerated his boasts:

> Whatever anyone dares to boast of—I am speaking as a fool—I also dare to boast of that. Are they Hebrews? So am I. Are they Israelites? So am I. Are they descendants of Abraham? So am I. Are they ministers of Christ? I am talking like a madman—I am a better one; with far greater labors, far more imprisonments, with countless floggings, and often near death. Five times I have received from the Jews the forty lashes minus one. Three times I was beaten with rods. Once I received a stoning. Three times I was shipwrecked; for a night and a day I was adrift at sea; on frequent journeys, in dangers from rivers, danger from bandits, danger from my own people, danger from Gentiles, danger in the city, danger in the wilderness, danger at sea, danger from false brothers and sisters; in toil and hardship, through many a sleepless night, hungry and thirsty, often without food, cold and naked. And besides other things, I am under daily pressure because of my anxiety for all the churches. Who is weak, and I am not weak? Who is made to stumble, and I am not indignant? (2 Corinthians 11:21–29)

He goes on a bit more with respect to one last trial (2 Corinthians 11:30–33). His point is to expose the absurdity of the boasting of his critics, but then his boasting becomes a bit more positive again:

> It is necessary to boast; nothing is to be gained by it, but I will go on to visions and revelations of the Lord. I know a person in Christ who fourteen years ago was caught up to the third heaven—whether in the body or out of the body I do not know; God knows—was caught up into Paradise and heard things that are not to be told, that no mortal is permitted to repeat. On behalf of such a one I will boast, but on my own behalf I will not boast, except of my weaknesses. But if I wish to boast, I will not be a fool, for I will be speaking the truth. But I refrain from it, so that no one may think better of me than what is seen in me or heard from me, even concerning the exceptional character of the revelations. (2 Corinthians 12:1–7a)

Paul also gives a more abbreviated version of his worldly virtues in his letter to the Philippians:

> If anyone has reason to be confident in the flesh, I have more: circumcised on the eighth day, a member of the people of Israel, of the tribe of Benjamin, a Hebrew born of Hebrews; as to the law, a Pharisee; as to zeal, a persecutor of the church; as to righteousness under the law, blameless. Yet whatever gain I had, these I have come to regard as loss because of Christ. More than that, I regard everything as loss because of the surpassing value of knowing Jesus Christ my Lord. (Philippians 3:4b–8a)

I have often been amused by preachers who can detail how many souls they have saved or how many people they have converted or brought to Christ. They're bragging. Preaching doesn't save any souls. Christ does. Conversion happens by the working of the Holy Spirit, not by the eloquence or the zeal of the evangelist. Yes, the Spirit may work through us, but God deserves the credit; we do not!

We have *this* ministry with Paul, who said:

> When I came to you, brothers and sisters, I did not come proclaiming the mystery of God to you in lofty words or wisdom. For I decided to know nothing among you except Jesus Christ, and him crucified. And I came to you in weakness and in fear and in much trembling. My speech and my proclamation were not with plausible words of wisdom, but with a demonstration of the Spirit and of power, so that your faith might rest not on human wisdom but on the power of God. (1 Corinthians 2:1–5)

Paul also said of "this ministry," "It is he whom we proclaim, warning everyone and teaching everyone in all wisdom, so that we may present everyone mature in Christ. For this I toil and struggle with all the energy that he powerfully inspires within me" (Colossians 1:28–29). Paul is like an instructor who hopes his students have truly gained the knowledge he has offered and will have become worthy of the headmaster's commendation.

Our ministry is as much that of witnesses to the power of God as it is service in His name. It is not wrong to keep a record of God's accomplishments, but we should not boast about them as if they were our own.

When our ability to lead is called into question, we need to remember the love God has for us. We need to remember that we serve the glorious purposes of Christ. It is not about us—it is about the Kingdom of God! It is wonderful when people catch the Spirit. But for some, as Paul said, it seems veiled.

> When one turns to the Lord, the veil is removed. Now the Lord is the Spirit, and wherever the Spirit of the Lord is there is freedom. And all of us, with unveiled faces, seeing the glory of the Lord as though reflected in a mirror, are being transformed into the same image from one degree of glory to another; for this comes from the Lord, the Spirit. (2 Corinthians 3:16–18)

It is then that Paul begins to speak of "this ministry." It is transformative. We know this because we are being transformed. There is something visionary in the inspiration it brings us. But "even if our gospel is veiled, it is veiled to those who are perishing. In their case the god of this world has blinded the minds of the unbelievers, to keep them from seeing the light of the gospel of the glory of Christ, who is the image of God" (2 Corinthians 4:3–4). With the unenlightened, sometimes the best we can do is let the light within us shine!

In Second Corinthians, chapter 5, Paul gave us a few more words about "this ministry:"

> From now on, therefore, we regard no one from a human point of view; even though we once knew Christ from a human point of view, we know him no longer in this way. So if anyone is in Christ there is a new creation: everything old has passed away; see, everything has become new! All this is from God, who reconciled us to himself through Christ, and has given to us the ministry of reconciliation; that is, in Christ God was reconciling the world to himself, not counting their trespasses against them, and entrusting the message of reconciliation to us. So we are ambassadors for Christ, since God is making his appeal through us; we entreat you on behalf of Christ, be reconciled to God. For our sake he made him to be sin who knew no sin, so that in him we might become the righteousness of God. (2 Corinthians 5:16–21)

We are not only to be ambassadors. Paul also felt a responsibility for those to whom he had taught Christ.

> I want you to know how much I am struggling for you, and for those in Laodicea, and for all who have not seen me face to face. I want their hearts to be encouraged and united in love, so that they may have all the riches of assured understanding and have the knowledge of God's

mystery, that is, Christ himself, in whom are hidden all the treasures of wisdom and knowledge. (Colossians 2:1–3)

The wonderful gift of faith, which is as much caught as taught, is filled with "riches." And Paul wants everyone whom he has taught to gain the blessing he knows.

We do not proclaim ourselves; we proclaim Jesus Christ as Lord and ourselves as your slaves for Jesus' sake. For it is the God who said, "Let light shine out of darkness," who has shone in our hearts to give the light of the knowledge of the glory of God in the face of Jesus Christ. (2 Corinthians 4:5–6)

How precious is the wonderful grace that fills our hearts and minds! But ... we are only "earthen vessels." (1 Corinthians 4:7 KJV)

Reflections on Psalm 23. *The Lord is my shepherd* (23:1a). Though pastors are often considered the shepherds of a flock, always remember that it is Jesus who is *the* shepherd. He is the good shepherd, our shepherd. Remember how He said, "I am the good shepherd. The good shepherd lays down his life for the sheep" (John 10:11).

We who are the paid servants of a congregation are ... sheepdogs! We chase after the flock and bark a lot.

Scriptures

Here are some relevant passages of scripture to inspire a deeper understanding of "the ministry" from the biblical point of view.

How beautiful upon the mountains are the feet of the messenger who announces peace, who brings good news, who announces salvation, who says to Zion, "Your God reigns." (Isaiah 52:7)

"I will give you as a light to the nations, that my salvation may reach to the ends of the earth." (Isaiah 49:6b)

Trust in the Lord with all your heart, and do not rely on your own insight. In all your ways acknowledge him, and he will make straight your paths. Do not be wise in your own eyes; fear the Lord and turn away from evil. It will be healing for your flesh and refreshment for your body. (Proverbs 3:5–8)

"Come to me all who are weary and are carrying heavy burdens, and I will give you rest. Take my yoke upon you, and learn from me; for I am gentle and humble in heart, and you will find rest for your souls. For my yoke is easy, and my burden is light." (Matthew 11:28–30)

"Those who love their life lose it, and those who hate their life in this world will keep it for eternal life. Whoever serves me must follow me, and where I am, there will my servant be also. Whoever serves me, the Father will honor." (John 12:25–26)

We have gifts that differ according to the grace given to us: prophecy, in proportion to faith; ministry, in ministering; the teacher, in teaching; the exhorter, in exhortation; the giver, in generosity; the leader, in diligence; the compassionate, in cheerfulness. (Romans 12:6–8)

Those who are taught the word must share in all good things with their teacher. (Galatians 6:6)

Each of us was given grace according to the measure of Christ's gift. (Ephesians 4:7)

I can do all things through him who strengthens me. (Philippians 4:13)

My God will fully satisfy every need of yours according to his riches in glory in Christ Jesus. (Philippians 4:19)

As God's chosen ones, holy and beloved, clothe yourselves with compassion, kindness, humility, meekness, and patience. Bear with one another and, if anyone has a complaint against another, forgive each other; just as the Lord has forgiven you, so you also must forgive. Above all, clothe yourselves with love, which binds everything together in perfect harmony. (Colossians 3:12–14)

Pay close attention to yourself and to your teaching; continue in these things, for in doing this you will save both yourself and your hearers. (1 Timothy 4:16)

God did not give us a spirit of cowardice, but rather a spirit of power and of love and of self-discipline. (2 Timothy 1:7)

Like good stewards of the manifold grace of God, serve one another with whatever gift each of you has received. (1 Peter 4:10)

Tend the flock of God that is in your charge, exercise oversight, not under compulsion but willingly, as God would have you do it not for sordid gain but eagerly. (1 Peter 5:2)

Since all these things are to be dissolved in this way, what sort of persons ought you to be in leading lives of holiness and godliness. (2 Peter 4:11)

WHAT TO DO

> Respect and affirm the integrity of "this ministry."
> Realize that pastors have earned their position.
> Revisit and reaffirm the experiences that brought you into "this ministry"—the ways God has "shone in our hearts."
> Stay true to your purpose.
> Think of how you have experienced the mixed blessings of this life.
> Think about things that have happened that cause you to doubt.
> Think about your diplomas. What can you show—boast about— to others that affirms your qualifications for being in the ministry.
> Examine your expectations of "this ministry." Are they appropriate? Or are they exaggerated or watered down?
> How are pastors more like sheepdogs than like shepherds?
> Don't lose heart!

Prayer

Almighty God, it's so sad knowing that the truth is veiled for those who are perishing. So I ask that my words be laser-like in order to penetrate the spiritual blindness that exists. And help me remember that it is by Your mercy that I have this ministry. So help me do what I can and speak what You've said in order to magnify Your grace, that the world may see it as clearly as possible. I ask this prayer in Jesus's name. Amen.

Song
Whispers and Teardrops

I'm in a maze that has no end;
It has no beginning, and I need a friend.
My name is my shadow; my image, a laugh.
A smile is my symbol—or my epitaph.
　There are whispers and teardrops, and sunrise-cold dew
　When you wander at nighttime to find something new.

I know where I've been, Lord, but where will I go?
Master of vigilance, open a door!
There I will enter, and there will I be
Part of the purpose of infinity.
　There are whispers and teardrops, and sunrise-cold dew
　When you wander at nighttime to find something new.

CHAPTER 2

We Have This Treasure

But we have this treasure in clay jars,
so that it may be made clear
that this extraordinary power
belongs to God and does not come from us.
2 Corinthians 4:7

We have treasure! Second Corinthians 4:7 and 13 say, "*We have this treasure in clay jars*" (emphasis mine) and "We have the same spirit of faith." This is the inspiration for the title of this chapter.

We are truly blessed! Not because we have acquired wealth or some form of abundance. Not because we have an excellent talent of some kind. Not because we are popular and loved or admired by great crowds. We are blessed because we are loved by God. We are enabled by His love to count the greatest blessing of all: that Jesus Christ is our Lord, that He loves us and died for our sins, that He has given us mercy and grace.

It is all too easy to take our blessings for granted when we have been offended by critics, undercut by those who feel they could do the job of ministry better than we can, or given negative feedback for our best efforts. We need to stay focused. We can choose what we think about:

> Whatever is true, whatever is honorable, whatever is just, whatever is pure, whatever is pleasing, whatever is commendable, if there is any excellence, and if there is anything worthy of praise, think about these things. Keep on doing the things that you have learned and received and heard and seen in me, and the God of peace will be with you. (Philippians 4:8–9)

Very little was remarkable about the clay jars often used to preserve important documents or letters. But think of the Dead Sea Scrolls: wonderful manuscripts that were kept in clay jars and discovered in caves near the Dead Sea in the 1940s. Many of these scrolls are among the earliest copies of scripture we now have, stored for safekeeping but forgotten over time. When discovered, they were able to confirm or inform contemporary and ongoing translations of the Bible. These large jars were simply the containers used to protect the scrolls. Even though time had had its way with the physical texts, many survived to shed light on the precious words of our faith.

We are like those earthen vessels: ordinary, yet containing the precious words of faith in our hearts and minds. Rarely do people know what we hold in our hearts because of our studies, our being immersed in God's word, and our devotional times of prayer, reading, and worship. It doesn't show outwardly, at least not obviously for some, but what we know is like a fire burning within us. Jeremiah said, "If I say, 'I will not mention him, or speak any more in his name,' then there is within me something like a burning fire shut up in my bones; I am weary with holding it in, and I cannot" (Jeremiah 20:9). Even though he had become a "laughingstock" (Jeremiah 20:7), and even though "the word of the Lord had become for me a reproach and derision all day long" (Jeremiah 20:8), Jeremiah still proclaimed the testimony that God had placed on his heart. He felt as though "the Lord is with me like a dread warrior" (Jeremiah 20:11).

We are shadows of that warrior! (For this image, I am indebted to the filmmaker Akira Kurosawa for the movie *Kagemusha* ["The Shadow Warrior"]). We may not be the real warrior, but we can be so like Jesus by imitating His ways and speaking His words that people will recognize the true Warrior in whose shadow we stand. We are not practicing pretense; we are not just playing a role; we are not being false or doing an impersonation. We are honoring the real Warrior by doing our best to be like him. We are shadow warriors!

Like Jeremiah, we can't keep it in. Paul said, "An obligation is laid on me, and woe to me if I do not proclaim the gospel!" (1 Corinthians 9:16). We are not to think of ourselves as having *earned* the Spirit of Christ, and yet we actually do have His Spirit. He endows us with His grace. We can be like Him as we strive for perfection. No, we are not *there* yet, but we press on (Philippians 3:12).

What is this treasure like? It's like something discovered that had been buried in the ground, but it's so special that we would sacrifice everything to buy that ground (Matthew 13:44). It is not something that can be stored away. It is stored in our hearts, and "where our treasure is there will our hearts be also" (Matthew 6:21).

Where is the truth? It may seem that it is in some written document, but in reality, it is in the deeds of those who live it. It is in the words of those who speak it. It in the hearts of those who trust it. We are keepers of the truth, "we are stewards of the mysteries of God," and we are "servants of Christ" (1 Corinthians 4:1).

When I think of the suffering of Christ—beaten, whipped, crowned with thorns, nailed to a cross, and executed—and how He endured it all for my benefit, my salvation, I am sometimes brought to tears. His extraordinary graciousness, given when it is I who deserve what He received, is overwhelming. It is a treasure so precious that I can't help but just gaze upon it at times. I need to recall it often because it is good medicine for my spirit, and I cherish it always.

I am reminded of the many words of encouragement in scripture regarding the treasure within me, such as:

> For the love of Christ urges us on, because we are convinced that one has died for all; therefore all have died. And he died for all, so that those who live might live no longer for themselves, but for him who died and was raised again. (2 Corinthians 5:14–15)

I love the words of assurance in Paul's letter to the Philippians:

I have learned to be content with whatever I have. I know what it is to have little, and I know what it is to have plenty. In any and all circumstances I have learned the secret of being well-fed and of going hungry, of having plenty and of being in need. I can do all things through him who strengthens me. (Philippians 4:11–13)

Reflections on Psalm 23. *I shall not want* (v. 1b). The New International Version says, "I lack nothing," translated in the New Century Version as "I have everything I need." By faith we discover the sufficiency of Christ. He is everything we need, and He is all we need. That's the secret!

We are enabled! There is a power within us by the Spirit of Christ that makes us almost indomitable. While we need to remember what keeps us going, we also need to ask ourselves what can stop us in our tracks. What stalls our engines? What puts a damper on our fires?

The biggest "damper" of all is failure. When we fail to hold someone's attention while we are offering gems of wisdom and truth, when we fail to see any hearts on fire with what ignites the fires within us, when the response is minimal to the invitations we offer to study, serve, or to support some need, nothing dims the light like ignoring it. Nothing holds us back like those who seem to be holding buckets of cold water over us, ready to put out our fires.

I have likened the ministry to the process of announcing a wonderful cure. People are often glad to know about the cure. People feel good because there *is* a cure. But they have to come forward to receive it. The cure is on the table; we can't force it upon anyone. They must want it for themselves. All we can do is be invitational and hope people respond. I don't like "hard-sell" evangelism—the kind filled with threats of condemnation for nonbelievers. When people are faithful out of fear, I believe something is missing. But when we can love someone into faith, it can be glorious.

I have mentioned a good friend who is a wonderful environmentalist and popular advocate and speaker. His message is not complicated, but it is desperately needed. He often confronts the indifference and lethargy of some of the people before whom he speaks. But there *is* an urgency. We need to stave off climate change as much as possible. He does not speak with threats about the earth's destruction, though I don't believe it would be wrong to, since we need to act quickly to change our course. He speaks with reason and encouragement. Still, people are not always willing to listen to reason. A time may come—too soon, perhaps—when he will be able to say (though I don't believe he will, as he is too gracious and not that arrogant), "I told you so." And I sometimes feel that a time will come when everyone who preaches the gospel of Christ will be able to say, "I told you so." But by then, it might be too late.

It is sad to think that the gospel is "veiled to those who are perishing" (2 Corinthians 4:3). At the same time, we are very conscious of the treasure we hold in the clay jars of our lives. An "extraordinary power" is working in us, but the "power belongs to God and does not come from us" (2 Corinthians 4:7b). We are only messengers, yes. But the message is extraordinary!

SCRIPTURES

Here are some relevant passages of scripture to inspire a deeper understanding of "the treasure" we have from the biblical point of view.

My child, if you accept my words and treasure up my commandments within you, making your ear attentive to wisdom and inclining your heart to understanding; if you indeed cry out for insight, and raise your voice for understanding; if you seek it like silver and search for it as for hidden treasures then you will understand the fear of the Lord and find the knowledge of God. (Proverbs 2:1–5)

Happy are those who find wisdom, and those who get understanding, for her income is better than silver, and her revenue better than gold. She is more precious than jewels, and nothing you desire can compare to her. (Proverbs 3:13–15)

In the house of the righteous is much treasure, but trouble befalls the income of the wicked. (Proverbs 15:16)

The human mind may devise many plans, but it is the purpose of the Lord that will be established. (Proverbs 19:21)

A good name is to be chosen rather than great riches (Proverbs 22:1)

Strive first for the kingdom of God and his righteousness, and all these things will be given to you. (Matthew 6:33)

Life is more than food, and the body more than clothing. (Luke 12:23)

Sell your possessions and give alms. Make purses for yourselves that do not wear out, an unfailing treasure in heaven, where no thief comes near and no moth destroys. For where your treasure is, there your heart will be also. (Luke 12:33–34)

I want their hearts to be encouraged and united in love, to that they may have all the riches of assured understanding and have the knowledge of God's mystery, that is, Christ himself, in whom are hidden all the treasures of wisdom and knowledge. (Colossians 2:2–3)

What to Do

> Be conscious of how the true treasures are divine, not earthly; spiritual, not worldly.
> Study God's Word. The treasure mine!
> Worship! Be a presence before God and others as an example of pure faith. You are a treasure for others to discover!
> Learn the secret of contentment.
> What is the "fire burning in your bones"? What is your passion?
> Think of how God is strengthening you right now.
> Ask yourself what enables the manifestations of the treasures in your heart.
> Become aware of the "dampers" in your life. How will you deal with them?

Prayer

Almighty God, help me remember that my truest treasures are still yet to come, and help me cherish Your Word in such a way that it is like precious jewels in my life. Give us all wisdom enough to know that worldly wealth is what is most illusive and that a life of faith gives the greatest abundance of all. I ask this prayer in Jesus's name. Amen.

POEM
To Treasure

You are feathers in the wind.
You are dreams when sleep won't end.
You're a gentle rolling sway,
And you are a relaxing day.

I hear the softness of some tune
And feel the color of the moon.
I see the rhythm of a fire
And know the warmth that you inspire.

There are dancers in the night;
There is beauty in our sight.
There is walking home alone
With the simple dreams I've known.

You are like the blessed time
When every word begins to rhyme.

CHAPTER 3

Afflicted but Not Crushed

⚭

To keep me from being too elated,
a thorn was given me in the flesh,
a messenger of Satan to torment me,
to keep me from being too elated.
Three times I appealed to the Lord about this,
that it would leave me,
but he said,
"My grace is sufficient for you, for power is made perfect in weakness."
So I will boast all the more gladly of my weaknesses,
so that the power of Christ may dwell in me.
Therefore I am content with weaknesses,
insults, hardships, persecutions, and calamities
for the sake of Christ,
for whenever I am weak, then I am strong.
(2 Corinthians 12:7b-10)

There is always something that will bring us down to earth. We all suffer from afflictions. They may not come until we have lived awhile. Youth does have its blessings, and our bodies seem to endure much. But everyone can get sick, catch a cold, face the flu … and we usually don't necessarily consider such things as "afflictions." They may seem more like little glitches. Still, they are wonderful signs of how the human body can overcome various distresses. Injuries happen, accidents occur, and trials come. But, as I've said before, every scar is a sign that we have risen above such "thorns." We have healed! We often recognize this truth, though, only in retrospect. While we are going through our afflictions, we can feel a bit "crushed."

Paul was in so much anguish from what he called "a thorn in his flesh" that he considered it to be "a messenger of Satan"! Sometimes, it may be exactly that. Paul saw it as something that kept him from being too quick to brag. It kept him from being "too elated." He felt like he could fly, but his wings were clipped.

Jesus has said, "In the world ye shall have tribulation: but be of good cheer; I have overcome the world" (John 16:33 KJV). To me, this means that when we have faith in Christ, we too can overcome. His grace is able to work in us, and we can rise above the afflictions of this world. Not only that, but we can even "rejoice in our sufferings" (Romans 5:3).

To be "afflicted, but not crushed" is to be conscious of both the reality of our suffering and the fact that it does not defeat us. Sadly, however, what we have to endure can take its toll. For one, it can keep us, as it did with Paul, from being too elated. There is always something that brings us down to earth.

At the same time, when we are subjected to afflictions, we learn over and over that we can indeed *endure* afflictions. "We are more than conquerors!" (Romans 8:37). Nothing can "separate us from the love of God in Christ Jesus our Lord" (Romans 8:39). This needs to be our posture in the world. When we are beaten, though, our posture doesn't always look perfect. We become a bit bent over. We can look as though we have just been punched in the gut. We don't quite look like conquerors. I'm sure Paul's "thorn" may have caused him to wince and to step somewhat haltingly. The good news is that we do recover. We can rise again. We are not crushed!

But what could it mean to be crushed? Well, if an army is crushed, the soldiers surrender, the white flags go up, and people would rather be alive as prisoners than die in a slaughter. To be crushed is to be close to death. Sometimes, being betrayed can crush us. I have known several friends who, felt "crushed" when a girlfriend or boyfriend broke up with them. They felt their love interests had betrayed their affections for someone else. Some of them were devastated … for a few days. But they soon realized that it wasn't the end. They would find someone new, eventually. It is different, however, when the one you love dies. You can be crushed by grief. Being crushed can feel like you can't go on. There can be an aloneness that is so heavy that it seems to squeeze the life right out of you. But with faith in Christ, we know we are not alone.

We can be crushed by humiliation, shame, disgrace, or embarrassment. We can feel crushed by guilt. Whatever brings us to our knees seems crushing at the time. But maybe being on your knees means it's time to pray!

When we remember that we are redeemed, lifted up, justified, and forgiven by God's grace in Jesus Christ, we begin to rediscover the treasures in life. Of course, it takes faith. But when it is our sinfulness that crushes us, or especially when we have lost faith, we need the grace of others, their reassurance, their love.

Long ago, as an interning chaplain in the Federal Corrections Institute in Englewood, Colorado, I became acquainted with inmates who had been incarcerated for their crimes. One way they dealt with this crushing defeat was with anger—at someone in particular, at some part of a "system" that worked contrary to their hopes and plans, or even at God. We often blame others for our circumstances. But many of the men had felt encouraged by their families, by their hope for returning to them and to a more honest life, and by a sense that their imprisonment was only temporary. One man told me that he felt hopeful just looking forward to his next meal, even though he felt that the food was lousy. Every little glimmer of hope, every next sunrise, every next hour, minute, or second can be an encouraging sign that bolsters our morale. But it takes resolve.

We are afflicted but not crushed!

Even when what afflicts us is the saddening indifference of some toward the gospel, our posture needs to be supported by the fact that *they* are making a choice. It is not necessarily about *our* shortcomings as messengers, or, our flaws as speakers, or even our lack of knowledge about some issue or other. We proclaim Jesus Christ, who was crucified, died, was buried, but who rose again! We, too, can rise again. New life is always right around the corner. Perhaps there is even a whole new path.

Be encouraged:

> Therefore, my beloved, be steadfast, immovable, always abounding in the work of the Lord, because you know that in the Lord your labor is not in vain. (1 Corinthians 15:58)

> Let us not grow weary in doing what is right, for we will reap at harvest time, if we do not give up. (Galatians 6:9)

> Those who wait for the Lord shall renew their strength, they shall mount up with wings like eagles, they shall run and not be weary, they shall walk and not faint. (Isaiah 40:31)

Reflections on Psalm 23. *He makes me lie down in green pastures; he leads me beside still waters; he restores my soul* (vs. 2–3a). We can look forward to the green pastures and still waters that will restore us. Sheep don't like flowing water. If they slip into a stream, with their thick wool and tiny feet, it is hard for them to swim. A good shepherd builds up an eddy, using stones from the creek bed, to create a nice, calm pool along the bank from which the lambs can slake their thirst. Nothing is more restorative than a nice cool, clear pond.

We need to know what can restore our souls. Our bodies too! One time I took my guitar down to the river, sat with my back against a tree, and just picked quiet, slow melodies on the strings. It was a peaceful setting, and the music was gentle. I was creative. Sometimes, being creative is exactly what we need. For some, it might be listening to music. It doesn't always have to be mellow. Depending on my mood, I like to crank up some good solid rock! Sometimes, in the past, I have gone for a nice, long, slow run.

Scriptures

Here are some relevant passages of scripture to inspire a deeper understanding of "afflictions" from the biblical point of view.

The afflicted shall eat and be satisfied; those who seek him shall praise the Lord. (Psalm 22:26)

Turn to me and be gracious to me, for I am lonely and afflicted. Relieve the troubles of my heart, and bring me out of my distress. Consider my affliction and my trouble, and forgive all my sins. (Psalm 25:16–18)

Many are the afflictions of the righteous, but the Lord rescues them from them all. (Psalm 34:19)

It was good for me that I was humbled, so that I might learn your statutes. (Psalm 119:71)

Do not fear, for I am with you, do not be afraid, for I am your God. (Isaiah 41:10)

When you pass through the waters, I will be with you; and through the rivers, they shall not overwhelm you. (Isaiah 43:2)

It was no messenger or angel but his presence that saved them; in his love and in his pity he redeemed them; he lifted them up and carried them all the days of old. (Isaiah 63:9)

I consider that the sufferings of this present time are not worth comparing with the glory about to be revealed to us. (Romans 8:18)

Blessed be the God and Father of our Lord Jesus Christ, the Father of mercies and the God of all consolation, who consoles us in all our afflictions, so that we may be able to console those who are in any affliction with the consolation with which we ourselves are consoled by God. (2 Corinthians 1:3–4)

Bear one another's burdens, and in this way you will fulfill the law of Christ. (Galatians 6:2)

Do not worry about anything, but in everything by prayer and supplication with thanksgiving let your requests be made known to God. (Philippians 4:6)

Are any among you suffering? They should pray. Are any cheerful? They should sing songs of praise. (James 5:13)

Whoever speaks must do so as one speaking the very words of God, whoever serves must do so with the strength that God supplies, so that God may be glorified in all things through Jesus Christ. To him belong the glory and the power forever and ever. Amen. (1 Peter 4:11)

What to Do

> Pray. In everything, let your requests be made known to God!
> Consider how God's power might be made perfect in our human weaknesses.
> Think about your scars, if you have any. Realize that they are a sign that your body healed from a wound there. What was it that wounded you?
> Think about the "thorns" in your life that have kept you from being too elated. What else brings you down to earth?
> Think about where you can go or what you can do in order for God to restore your soul.
> Consider what could happen to bring you to your knees. Plan now how you might pray while you're there.
> Compare your suffering with the glory that will be revealed to us. Not to minimalize your suffering now, but realize that it is nothing beside God's glory. How does what you suffer help you identify with the sufferings of Christ?
> Think about what enables you to "mount up with wings like eagles." What enables you to "run and not grow weary"?

Prayer

Almighty God, I am weakened by my afflictions, but I am empowered by Your grace to rise above them. Let that remarkable reality permeate my being and fill my mind. If there is a purpose in my suffering, help me learn it. If there is grace sufficient for my needs, let me trust it. And if there is mercy in my future, let me believe it now. I ask this prayer in Jesus's name. Amen.

POEMS
Evening of Change

I don't know, but now it seems
To be a vision of my dreams,
For tenderly God's comfort came
And leaving didn't feel the same.

Everything my heart has gained
Has never fully been explained.
But I think I've learned a bit about
Casting off my fear and doubt
To let the freedom there should be
Quit hiding and then come to me.

I'm looking now at all I know,
And I believe it's gonna grow.
But what I thought my dreams would find
Is different, 'cause I've changed my mind.

For Mary G.

Laughter is the sound of souls—
The sign of all creation's goals,
The love of life that lets us be
Children of God, alive and free.
And filling us from full to flood,
It's pouring forth to warm our blood
And leave us with a simple smile
That wants to stay there for a while.

And if I could only find its source
And follow on its happy course,
I think I know what I would find:
A thousand dreams would be combined,

'Cause laughter's like a smile come true—
It even makes our hearts seem new!

CHAPTER 4

Perplexed but Not Driven to Despair

❧

I think that God has exhibited us apostles as last of all,
as though sentenced to death,
because we have become a spectacle to the world,
to angels and to mortals.
We are fools for the sake of Christ,
but you are wise in Christ.
We are weak, but you are strong.
You are held in honor, but we in disrepute.
To this present hour we are hungry and thirsty,
and we grow weary from the work of our own hands.
When reviled, we bless;
when persecuted, we endure;
when slandered, we speak kindly.
We have become like the rubbish of the world, the dregs of all things,
to this very day.
1 Corinthians 4:9–13

> We are treated as imposters, and yet are true;
> as unknown, and yet are well known;
> as dying, and see—we are alive;
> as punished, and yet not killed;
> as sorrowful, yet always rejoicing;
> as poor, yet making many rich;
> as having nothing, and yet possessing everything.
> 2 Corinthians 6:8b-10

There is a paradox in a life of ministry. There are wonderful blessings, but there are harsh trials. And it may not always be a matter of either/or: there is often a mixture. Life is indeed, again, a mixed blessing. We try to lead, and nobody follows. We try to rally the troops, and no one rises to the cause. We try to stimulate the hearts and minds of those we serve, and no one seems enlightened. What we do can leave us quite perplexed, confused, dizzy.

We may appeal to the intellect of some and to the emotions of others. Either way, we might be mocked for intellectualizing faith or for being too manipulative by tugging on heartstrings. Paul wanted to be all things to all people, but that's just not possible—without faith. Paul's motive was "that I might by all means save some. I do it all for the sake of the gospel, so that I may share in its blessings" (1 Corinthians 22–23).

> Though I am free with respect to all, I have made myself a slave to all, so that I might win more of them. To the Jews I became as a Jew, in order to win Jews. To those under the law I became as one under the law (though I myself am not under the law) so that I might win those under the law. To those outside the law I became as one outside the law (though I am not free from God's law but am under Christ's law) so that I might win those outside the law. To the weak I became weak, so that I might win the weak. (1 Corinthians 9:19–21a)

I don't believe Paul was compromising his integrity. Rather, he was relating his message to those who needed to hear it. I imagine it may have been very confusing at times, for Paul himself, as well as for his hearers. "We are perplexed but not driven to despair" (2 Corinthians 4:8b).

When I began my ministry, I imagined people would catch my fire and the blazes would spread. I was naive. I didn't realize that many laypeople were the spiritual fire department, ready to maintain a status quo rather than change their lives, let alone hope to change the world. The big issue back in 1982 was the tremendous buildup of nuclear arms and the idea of a nuclear freeze—putting a halt to building more bombs, as we already had enough to destroy the world a few times over! Sadly, governments are still creating more bombs, and the "freeze" soon melted away. But what was obvious to me was not so obvious to the churches I served. I was even encouraged once to go to Russia and preach my message there. I explained that that was not my calling.

The good news was that I was not alone. Many other like-minded "radicals" weren't too far away. Following Paul's example of being all things to all people, do we become hawks to the hawks, hippies to the hippies, or morally loose to the decadent? Of course not. But we do need to understand where they are coming from. We need to identify enough with others to know why they think the way they do. Very perplexing!

Now even though life may in fact be very perplexing, we need not despair, though confusion may do that to us. It can be hard to find direction, hard to sort out goals and know how to begin. But we are to begin with Jesus Christ. He is our guide and our goal. His Word is our compass. His cross is our journey. We walk by faith and not by sight (2 Corinthians 5:7). And inasmuch as it may seem impossible to get others to catch the vision, when we are able to set our sights on where we want to go, others will see that in us and hopefully realign their sights.

I am challenged by the word "driven" in 2 Corinthians 4:8. Often the perplexing realities of life can, in fact, "drive" us to despair. Like distractions along the road, they make us look away from where we are going. Well, keep your eyes on the road. To what *do* we pay attention? When our purpose is to be true, we will know we are not impostors. When we are treated as "unknown," we need to make our purpose better known. Though we are treated as though we are dying, we need to reveal the new life we have by faith in Christ. When we are made sorrowful, we can still rejoice! We may be poor, but we know what the true riches are, and that is what we want to proclaim. We might seem to have nothing, but we possess the important things: faith, hope, and love.

> When reviled, we bless; when persecuted, we endure; when slandered, we speak kindly. We have become like the rubbish of the world, the dregs of all things, to this very day. (1 Corinthians 4:12–13)

We are not mired in this world, though. Our citizenship is in heaven (Philippians 3:20). Part of what is so perplexing is that we're not *there* yet. We are ambassadors here, now. But like any ambassador in a foreign land, we represent the land that is our true home. We are part of the kingdom of God. We may never see the harvest of our dreams, but we will still plant the seeds!

Part of the problem, however, is that even though we are not crushed, even though we are not driven to despair, we can still feel persecuted.

Reflections on Psalm 23. *He leads me in right paths for his name's sake.* (v. 3b) When John Wesley felt as through his faith was lacking, he was told, "Preach faith until you have it, and then, when you have it, you will preach faith!" Following a good path, a path of righteousness, can feel good. It can improve our mood and stir our hearts. Reflecting on what is "right" and "righteous" in our journeys can help us sort things out. Grow. Spiritual growth can include going through dark times, confusing days, or empty hours. But we can still "preach faith." The more we do some things, the more they become natural habits.

SCRIPTURES

Here are some relevant passages of scripture to inspire a deeper understanding of being "perplexed" from the biblical point of view.

This book of the law shall not depart out of your mouth; you shall meditate on it day and night, so that you may be careful to act in accordance with all that is written in it. For then you shall make your way prosperous, and then you shall be successful. (Joshua 1:8)

Cast your burden on the Lord, and he will sustain you; he will never permit the righteous to be moved. (Psalm 55:22)

You will keep him in perfect peace whose mind is stayed on you; because he trusts in you. (Isaiah 26:3 NKJV)

I will lead the blind on a road they do not know; by paths they have not known I will guide them. (Isaiah 42:16)

"Come to me, all you that are weary and are carrying heavy burdens, and I will give you rest. Take my yoke upon you, and learn from me; for I am gentle and humble in heart, and you will find rest for your souls. For my yoke is easy, and my burden is light." (Matthew 11:28–30)

"Peace I leave with you; my peace I give to you. I do not give to you as the world gives. Do not let your hearts be troubled, and do not let them be afraid." (John 14:27)

The peace of God, which surpasses all understanding, will guard your hearts and your minds in Christ Jesus. (Philippians 4:7)

Cast all your anxieties on him, because he cares for you. (1 Peter 5:7)

Now to him who is able to keep you from falling, and to make you stand without blemish in the presence of his glory with rejoicing, to the only God our savior, through Jesus Christ our Lord, be glory, majesty, power, and authority, before all time and now and forever. Amen. (Jude 24)

WHAT TO DO

> ‣ Trust. God's ways are perfect even when we don't understand them.
> ‣ Be a blessing. God makes us a blessing so that we might bless others!
> ‣ Practice the Golden Rule: do to others what you would want them to do to you.
> ‣ Think of a time when you tried to rally the troops and no one came to the cause. How did you feel? What did you do?

> ➤ Consider the ways "the ministry" can be confusing. How does that affect you?
> ➤ Realize that you are not alone in your efforts. How have you discovered this?
> ➤ Think of how God's Word can be like a compass for you.
> ➤ Remember that as ambassadors for Christ, we represent the holy, the divine, the perfect. We represent God.

PRAYER

O God, my guide and my guard, lead me in the direction You would have me go, and please go with me. I will trust You even when I can't tell whether or not You are there. I will immerse myself in Your Word so that it can be my compass and my hope. However confusing this world becomes to me, help me remember Your purpose and Your promises. I ask this prayer in Jesus's name. Amen.

POEMS
Perplexed

You fill the absences of light;
You are the emptiness of night.
You are the color of the unknown,
And you're the place to be alone.

I've seen some shadows in my mind;
I've seen fear and loss combined.
I am inside looking out
At the questions all about.

There are fears that many find,
Yet there's a tenderness behind
The shallow comfort you can share
whenever fear is never there.

Perhaps you are a soft opaque
Once pierced, there's no more fears to break

Loneliness

You are empty, but you are free:
You're the deepness of a barren sea;
You're the silence in abandoned song;
You're the dream of lost-and-gone.

I have seen you set apart;
I have felt you in my heart.
I have heard you in a breath
Of longing and in new-love's death.

There's something like a ghost behind
The farthest corners of my mind
That stays when you will try to sleep
And seems to make your presence keep.

You are a poetic time
When there are no more words that rhyme.

CHAPTER 5

Persecuted but Not Forsaken

Now, you have observed my teaching, my conduct, my aim in life,
my faith, my patience, my love, my steadfastness,
my persecutions,
and my suffering the things that happened to me
in Antioch, Iconium, and Lystra.
What persecutions I endured!
Yet the Lord rescued me from all of them.
Indeed, all who want to live a godly life in Christ Jesus
will be persecuted.
2 Timothy 3:10–12

Our Lord said, "Blessed are you when people revile you and persecute you and utter all kinds of evil against you falsely on my account. Rejoice and be glad, for your reward is great in heaven, for in the same way they persecuted the prophets who were before you" (Matthew 5:11–12). It is awkward to think of persecution as being a blessing, but this is one of the great paradoxes of faith. Persecution is another of those things we did not sign up for. But it happens. And I'm sorry.

In ancient Antioch in Asia Minor, one Sabbath day Paul preached a powerful sermon in the synagogue that pleased both the Jews and the Gentile converts to Judaism (Acts 13:14–41). After hearing him, they asked him to come again the next Saturday. "The next sabbath, the whole city gathered to hear the word of the Lord. But the Jewish leaders were jealous (because of the crowds) and contradicted what Paul was saying" (Acts 13:44–45). Paul and Barnabas said that their rejection left them no choice: "We are going to the Gentiles. For the Lord has commanded us saying, 'I have set you as a light for the Gentiles, so that you may bring salvation to the ends of the earth'" (vs. 46–47). The Gentiles were glad to hear this, "but the Jews incited the devout women of high standing and the leading men of the city, and stirred up persecution against Paul and Barnabas, and drove them out of the region" (v. 50). So they decided to go on to Iconium and "were filled with joy and with the Holy Spirit" (v. 52).

In Iconium, their message drew "great numbers of both Jews and Greeks" to become believers, "but unbelieving Jews stirred up the Gentiles and poisoned their minds against the brothers" (Acts 14:1, 2). Paul and Barnabas hung in there until "when an attempt was made … to mistreat them and to stone them, the apostles learned of it and fled" (vs. 4–6).

In Lystra (Acts 14:8–20), a disabled man heard Paul speak. Paul saw that he had faith to be healed, and he called on him to stand. The people of Lystra were so impressed when a healing occurred that they thought that "the gods had come down to us in human form!" (Acts 14:11). Well, Paul was not Hermes, and Barnabas was not Zeus. They did all they could to restrain the priest of Zeus and the crowds from sacrificing to them (v.18). It was then that some contradictory Jews from Antioch and Iconium stirred things up, and "they stoned Paul, and dragged him out of the city, supposing he was dead" (v.19). Good news: he revived! And on they went.

They retraced their journey back through Iconium and Antioch, encouraging those who believed to continue in the faith, saying, "It is through many persecutions that we must enter the kingdom of God" (Acts 14:22).

These were not the only places where Paul and other witnesses were persecuted—they *were* persecuted, but not forsaken. Paul had been stoned! They (the contradictory Jews) thought he was dead. Either he wasn't and he was healed, or he experienced a quick resurrection. God was working in Paul's life. Later, in his letter to the Romans, Paul said, "We know that all things work together for good for those who love God, who are called according to his purpose" (8:28).

That means even persecutions can work for God's purposes. It may not seem like they are "working" when we are going through them, but we need to trust God's plans. Whatever we go through, even though in our minds it might not seem like God's will, we are experiencing the manifestation of God's kingdom. Even God's Son was persecuted! Being persecuted can help us identify with Christ. We want to suffer with Him in order to rise with Him (Romans 6:5).

When we are being persecuted, it usually means that someone is not only against us but is malicious toward us. They have forsaken you; they won't believe anything good about you; they will malign you, ridicule you, and reject you. They mean evil against you. Often they don't let up, even when others defend your reputation. These people can be downright vindictive. Often they have little remorse even when their disenchantment is disruptive and damaging to the congregation. They may never pursue physical violence, but certainly their words can be harmful or at least hurtful. I remember how one pastor said, sadly, that "you can only bleed so much." But someone had been just unrelenting.

In his book *Clergy Killers: Guidance for Pastors and Congregations Under Attack* (Westminster Press, 1997), G. Lloyd Rediker researched and conducted interviews on this subject. It was hard for me to believe how many experiences he came up with. Rediker focuses on how to deal with "difficult" people: arbitration, confrontation, deliberation, compromise. I won't get into these ideas here, but I can say that, obviously, these people can't just be ignored. I have appealed to the vision of Christ for us in sermons and other messages such as my Pastor's Notes in the church newsletter. Most people will remember that they are supposed to be kind and loving. And when it is revealed to them that they have been unkind or unloving, they will apologize or at least lighten up a bit. The damage they do to the whole congregation needs to be amended sometimes. Or, they just need to stop being so negative.

A simple example (and a tame one) in my life had to do with my ministry beyond the congregation I was paid to serve. Nothing I was doing was bad, and I considered it all a part of my ministry. In the community, I was a leader of the high school's drug abuse prevention program; I was involved in a local civic group, the community's clergy leadership, and a criminal justice program in the annual conference; I led an anti-gambling program in our county; I led the County Cluster of United Methodist Clergy … I could go on a bit, (I am talking like a madman! [2 Corinthians 12:23b]), but that's enough.

"You're sure doing a lot of non-Church stuff!" one of the members of my congregation remarked.

I asked this person how many extra meetings she thought I had in order to be so involved. "What am I allowed to do with my 'free time'? Isn't my involvement in the community good for our congregation?" I felt that this person was just trying to find fault with what I was doing. "Did I shirk any responsibilities I had with our congregation?"

I suggested I log my hours for the church and my hours for the "extra" stuff. When I did so for one month, everyone realized that I was very obviously doing the "job" for which I was being paid. And that the "extra" stuff, which took up about ten hours a month, was good for the church because "our" pastor was seen as involved in the community.

With respect to whatever ways people can find fault, it often says as much about their distorted expectations of a pastor as it does about their experiences of ministry. By that, I mean perhaps they had negative experiences with previous pastors or were acquainted with the shortcomings of clergy in other congregations.

Another complaint leveled against me toward the end of my ministry in the United Methodist Church was that I was unavailable because I had been working at home more. But I worked at home because of my wife's disability. I had shared this in a newsletter and said that people were welcome to contact me at home if they needed to see me. I would even make them a cup of tea. I *was* available. The pastor's home is not off-limits to the members of the congregation. I have seldom claimed a day off. That doesn't mean I never took time off, but I was never unavailable.

I recognize that these examples of "persecution" are extremely mild. And yes, petty criticism and fault-finding are a form of persecution. There's no need to talk about any of the mean-spirited attitudes and words leveled at me during my career—I don't want anyone to look bad. But I did challenge one man for how mean-spirited he had suddenly become. He eventually apologized. The challenge, however, is that things can escalate from pettiness to abusiveness fairly quickly with some people.

But we are not forsaken! Never by God, and seldom by those who like and respect us. Still, persecutors can be destructive. Which leads us to the next chapter!

Reflections on Psalm 23. *Even though I walk through the darkest valley, I fear no evil; for you are with me; your rod and your staff—they comfort me* (v. 4). When God is with us, that sufficiency steps up and reminds us that we are not alone. There is nothing to fear. The rod and staff of the shepherd are comforting signs for the flock. With them the shepherd can ward off predators, and with them he can rescue a lamb that gets stuck in a hole or in a bush or is sinking in a stream. The staff can also be used to shoo away snakes or other dangerous beasts that might lurk in the meadow. Remember, the shepherd goes ahead of the flock, leading them on the right paths.

SCRIPTURES

Here are some relevant passages of scripture to inspire a deeper understanding of being "persecuted" from the biblical point of view.

Be strong and bold, have no fear or dread of them, because it is the Lord your God who goes with you, he will not fail you or forsake you. (Deuteronomy 31:6)

God is our refuge and strength, a very present help in trouble. (Psalm 46:1)

You are the light of the world. A city built on a hill cannot be hid. (Matthew 5:14)

If the world hates you, be aware that it hated me before it hated you. (John 15:18)

Bless those who persecute you; bless and do not curse them. (Romans 12:14)

At my first defense no one came to my support, but all deserted me. May it not be counted against them! But the Lord stood by me and gave me strength, so that through me the message might be fully proclaimed and all the Gentiles might hear it. So I was rescued from the lion's mouth. (2 Timothy 4:16–17)

Therefore, since we are surrounded by so great a cloud of witnesses, let us also lay aside every weight and the sin that clings so closely, and let us run with perseverance, the race that is set before us, looking to Jesus the pioneer and perfecter of our faith, who for the sake of the joy that was set before him endured the cross, disregarding its shame, and has taken his seat at the right hand of God. (Hebrews 12:1–2)

Even if you do suffer for doing what is right, you are blessed. Do not fear what they fear, and do not be intimidated, but in your hearts sanctify Christ as Lord. (1 Peter 3:14–15a)

Blessed is anyone who endures temptation. Such a one has stood the test and will receive the crown of life that the Lord has promised to those who love him. (James 1:12)

What to Do

> First of all, do not fear. It will seem natural, though, to feel disappointed that the good news you preach and teach will be rejected by some.

> Think about what the reward might be for being persecuted. What? Yes: it says in the Beatitudes that there is a reward for being persecuted (Matthew 5:12).

> Think about why jealousy or envy might raise resistance to your message. How do people usually react to the good news of the gospel?

> Expect some degree of persecution, or at least resistance and rejection.

> Think about how persecution can be "a manifestation of God's kingdom."

> Think about how someone's fault-finding might say more about that person and their distorted expectations than about your faults.

> Think about ways God can be a refuge in your life.

PRAYER

Dear Heavenly Lord, You truly are a refuge. You are like shade from the burning sun of fault-finding. Cover me when I feel persecuted. Give me grace to love those who harbor any kind of ill will against me. Help me remember that what they are expressing might say more about them than it does about me. Still, help me be patient as I try to understand them. Help me be kind when they are unkind. And give me grace to be bold in the face of persecution as I proclaim Your Word. I ask this prayer in Jesus's name. Amen.

SONG
Windy

You feel your soul a-thunder,
But you don't know what you feel.
Your heart begins to wonder,
And you wonder if it's real.
You watch the wind in sorrow;
You feel it rain but then
You're hoping that tomorrow
It will never rain again.

> You better keep your soul, my child:
> Don't lose it like the wind that lost the sail,
> 'Cause even when the course is mild,
> The sunshine you've been looking for can fail.

You're looking for a sunrise,
But you just don't watch the sky.
You live as if the wind had eyes,
And the rainbows pass you by.
You don't know what you're feeling
When they tell you what is best,
But still you know they're trying,
And you think that you've been blessed.

So young and yet so lonely!
And the feeling lingers on.
Maybe you are only
Just awaiting some new dawn.

You better keep your soul, my child:
Don't lose it like the wind that lost the sail,
'Cause even when the wind is mild,
The sunshine you've been looking for can fail.

When are you gonna wander,
And where are you gonna start?
Don't wait too much longer,
'Cause it's windy in my heart.

CHAPTER 6

Struck Down but Not Destroyed

When they heard these things,
they became enraged and ground their teeth at Stephen.
But filled with the Holy Spirit,
he gazed into heaven
and saw the glory of God and Jesus standing at the right hand of God.
"Look," he said, "I see the heavens opened
and the Son of Man standing at the right hand of God!"
But they covered their ears,
and with a loud shout all rushed together against him.
Then they dragged him out of the city
and began to stone him,
and the witnesses laid their coats at the feet of a young rabbi named Saul.
While they were stoning Stephen, he prayed,
"Lord, do not hold this sin against them."
When he had said this, he died.
Acts 7:54–60

That day a severe persecution began against the church in Jerusalem.
Acts 8:1b

Suddenly it was a crime to be a Christian! In the future, the severity of that crime would become a part of the culture in Rome. In AD 64, the city of Rome suffered a terrible fire. The emperor Nero (reigned AD 54–68) blamed its cause on the Christians. Brave Christians were arrested and thrown into the arena to entertain civilians by being devoured by lions or used as targets by gladiators. Some were doused with pitch, and their bodies were set on fire to light the night. Others were simply executed or tortured to death. But many of these men and women were not very "entertaining." They just let themselves be killed. They had a peace about them that welcomed death, because they knew that their death was their entry into God's eternal kingdom.

Persecution is bad. Though we know we're not forsaken, our earthly bodies can be destroyed. The good news is that our souls cannot. We can be struck down, but we will rise again. Always having a vision of the resurrection before us can give us a perspective about death that the world cannot understand.

With Paul, we become able to say, "To me, living is Christ and dying is gain" (Philippians 1:21). Paul proclaimed, "It is my eager expectation and hope that I will not be put to shame in any way, but that by my speaking with all boldness, Christ will be exalted now as always in my body, whether by life or by death" (Philippians 1:20).

So how can we exalt God in our death? My first answer: finish the race! Paul told Timothy:

> "I am already being poured out as a libation, and the time
> of my departure has come. I have fought the good fight, I
> have finished the race, I have kept the faith. From now on
> there is reserved for me the crown of righteousness which
> the Lord, the righteous judge, will give me on that day,
> and not only to me but also to all who have longed for his
> appearing" (2 Timothy 4:6–8)

Such confidence! We need to trust that the One who does not forsake us will also complete us when we die. It may be horribly sad to be destroyed by death, but it is wonderfully glorious to be welcomed in eternity.

We can also exalt God in our death by leaving a legacy. I'm not just talking about leaving an inheritance, though there is absolutely nothing wrong with that. I'm talking about your personal legacy. For what will you be remembered? What will people say about your life? Did your light shine for those who knew you? Did people see Christ through you? How will you have faced the end of your life?

Questions like these are awkward for many people. Our culture is so immersed in the idea of "living for today" that we seem not to care about the future, let alone about our eternal destiny.

The movie *The Bucket List* came out in 2008. It is about two old guys who made lists of the things they wanted to do before they died or "kicked the bucket." Well, in spring of 2022, I had completed my bucket list except for one last thing: getting to see the Grand Canyon. I had wanted to see it for decades, and then I finally did. Now I feel as though I have fulfilled my hopes for myself.

The one thing I can't really accomplish is building the anti-gravity car! My secrets will not go to the grave with me, though. I will leave them as a legacy … elsewhere.

But the Grand Canyon … wow! I wrote a poem about it.

At the Canyon

I journeyed to the canyon's rim, and my heart was quickly filled
With awe and wonder and a joy that gladly was instilled
So deep within I had to ask if I was really here.
It was as if perfection's power had quietly come near.

But it was I who got to gaze in reverence at the sight
Of this oldest of sensations that had caught Creation's light.
I saw myself astounded, standing on the canyon floor,
Glancing upward with the thought, *I could not ask for more.*

My dreams were filled; I was complete, and I was blown away
By beauty and by something like an overwhelming sway
Of grace and everlasting truth, of super unstained bliss,
And in my mind I simply thought that heaven was like this.

And now my heart was happy and my life was almost through.
Just one more thing was still undone: coming home to You!

The awesomeness of the Grand Canyon filled me, as I knew it would, with a sense of wonder so pure and an admiration so sweet that I can't help but thank God for all that has been created. This world is an incredible place. And I am glad to behold what God has made. Millions of people have seen the canyon, and I am only one of them. But I was drawn to it simply because … it's so grand! I wonder what the first humans to see it might have felt. It is more than just a wonderful sight. It is like a holy place where anyone can go to face their puniness in the grand scheme of things and to witness their insignificance before the mighty forces that made something so immense. Mountains do that for me as well. So do shorelines, sunrises and sunsets, forests, and streams. But the canyon is just so extraordinary that I felt just ordinary before it. But I also felt as though I had received a gift. It was given to me, to all of us, to behold.

Behold the power of God, the glory of God's grace, the perfection of God's love. These are things that cannot be destroyed, and we can treasure them. I have beheld the greatest wonder of all. I have beheld the grace of God. It actually completed me long ago. I know this now. Still, I am glad to have seen what my earthly eyes have seen.

Strike me down. It doesn't matter if my earthly body is destroyed. The part of me that will live on is far greater than anything my earthly eyes have beheld. I have Jesus Christ. And He is grand! "Behold," Stephen said, "I see the heavens opened and the Son of Man standing at the right hand of God!" (Acts 7:56). May this be our vision too.

If you are ever struck down, remember those Grand Canyon moments that can lift you up. But even better, remember that Jesus Christ died to take away your sin. Remember, "It is the God who said, 'Let light shine out of darkness' who has shone in our hearts to give the light of the knowledge of the glory of God in the face of Jesus Christ" (2 Corinthians 4:6).

Reflecting on Psalm 23. *You prepare a table before me in the presence of my enemies* (v. 5a). The flock trusts the shepherd for its safety and well-being. Sometimes it is just the sound or scent of their shepherd that is so reassuring. But because a good pasture is so directly connected to their shepherd, the sheep see him as their meal ticket. They are fed by virtue of the shepherd's guidance. That table includes the banquet of abundance we all can receive.

SCRIPTURES

Here are some relevant passages of scripture to inspire a deeper understanding of being "struck down" from the biblical point of view.

Truly the eye of the Lord is on those who fear him, on those who hope in his steadfast love, to deliver their soul from death, and to keep them alive in famine. (Psalm 34:18–19)

Blessed be the Lord, who daily lifts us up; God is our salvation. (Psalm 68:19)

Surely there is a future, and your hope will not be cut off. (Proverbs 23:18)

But all things considered, this is an advantage for a land: a king for a plowed field. The lover of money will not be satisfied with money; nor the lover of wealth, with gain. This also is vanity. (Ecclesiastes 4:9–10)

Surely I know the plans I have for you, says the Lord, plans for welfare and not for harm, to give you a future with hope. Then when you call upon me and come and pray to me, I will hear you. When you search for me, you will find me; if you seek me with all your heart, I will let you find me, says the Lord, and I will restore your fortunes and gather you from all the nations and all the places I have driven you, says the Lord, and I will bring you back to the place from which I sent you into exile. (Jeremiah 29:11–15)

Do not rejoice over me, O my enemy; when I fall, I shall rise; when I sit in darkness, the Lord will be a light to me. (Micah 7:8)

"The thief comes only to steal and kill and destroy. I came that they might have life, and have it abundantly." (John 10:10)

Consider him who endured such hostility against himself from sinners, so that you may not grow weary or lose heart. (Hebrews 12:3)

What to Do

> - Do not lose heart. God is with you.
> - Think of how dying is gain for the believer.
> - Remember those things that have enlivened your soul, as the Grand Canyon did mine, and let them continue to inspire you.
> - Think about what your legacy might be.
> - Create a bucket list, if you haven't already. If you have, review it. What do you want to do before you "kick the bucket"?
> - Fight the good fight. Finish the race! Keep the faith (2 Timothy 4:7).
> - Think about what it is that "completes" you.
> - Think about what you believe God's plans for you might be.

Prayer

O God, my strength and my salvation, I am broken; I am wounded; I am struck down. But by Your grace, I am not destroyed … yet. Uphold me with Your love, comfort me with Your peace, and revive me by Your power. I ask that You would bless those who might intend to strike me down. Give to them such light that they will see the darkness of their thinking and so seek the grace that can bless us all. I ask this prayer in Jesus's name. Amen.

Song
Broken Throne

O battered, beaten, broken throne,
    Why do you still protect me now?
    The sweat is heavy on my brow,
And I would leave you all alone.

Just like a cracked and bleeding chalice
    Spilling forth its sour wine,
    Your destiny is death; but mine,
Desertion of this holy palace.

I will be looking back someday,
    But I would be a drifting cloud,
    And then, perhaps, I might be proud.
But 'fore I leave, I wish to pray.

O God, the time for me to leave has come.
    Pray, lead me straight upon Thy sight.
Remaining here my dreams will numb
    And seem as though a fading light.

Crack Thy whip of faith on me,
    And spill me from my heartless throne.
Pour me to Thy righteous sea,
    And leave me not to be alone.
I cannot rule this ill demesne
    With vain corruption still at hand
And fight the evils of my reign
    When half to full alone I stand.
        Pray, my Lord, please, bring me home
        Or lead me where no others roam.

POEM
To Comfort

You are wine drops. You're a long embrace.
You're softness from a fireplace.
You're the moonlight in a quiet sky.
You're like a wordless lullaby

I have felt you on a windy day,
But somehow you have never stayed.
But when I prayed beside my bed,
I knew that you were just ahead.

There is silence. There is sleep.
There is a dream I want to keep.
There was a heartbeat I have had
That made me know that I was glad

Because I knew that you were there,
And I was comforted by care.

CHAPTER 7

Carrying the Death of Jesus

If any want to become my followers,
let them deny themselves
and take up their cross
and follow me.
Matthew 16:24

One of my favorite passages of scripture is Galatians 2:19b-20: "I have been crucified with Christ; and it is no longer I who live, but it is Christ who lives in me. And the life I now live in the flesh I live by faith in the Son of God who loved me and gave himself for me."

This and Christ's words about self-denial and cross-bearing complement each other wonderfully. And they help to magnify Paul's encouraging words about carrying the death of Jesus in our bodies. Becoming a soldier is, in many ways, a process of self-denial. You lose your personal identity to the degree that you are equal to everyone else. You all wear the same clothes, the uniform; have similar haircuts; march together; and follow very strict orders ... together. Your life is not about you; it becomes totally devoted to your country, your government, your flag, and your commanding officer. You do exactly what they say. You follow your leader into battle not for your own purposes but for the purpose of the cause you are fighting. Your purpose becomes that of those who give the orders.

Jesus calls his followers to deny themselves. His purpose becomes our purpose, and we must follow his Word. It is no longer we who live, but Christ who lives in us (Galatians 2:20). But that happens when we are "crucified with Christ" (2:19b). The cross was the instrument of Jesus's sacrifice for the sins of the world. We take up that purpose of sacrifice in our lives. Our ministry is one of servanthood. We are servants of the cross, as we are servants of Christ. We should never be surprised that we might suffer for the cause.

Our fight, however, "is not against enemies of blood and flesh, but against the rulers, against the authorities, against the cosmic powers of this present darkness, against the spiritual forces of evil in the heavenly places" (Ephesians 6:12). When we are persecuted by people in this world, they are often participants in "this present darkness," even though they may not know it, and even though they might not willingly do so.

Paul spoke of how we are "always carrying in the body the death of Jesus, that the life of Jesus may also be made visible in our bodies. For while we live, we are always being given up to death for Jesus' sake, so that the life of Jesus may be made visible in our mortal flesh. So death is at work in us, but life in you" (2 Corinthians 4:10–11). Although Paul is being very personal in this verse, very autobiographical, he is still including everyone in his sphere of ministry. Our scars are visible reminders of our woundedness. Our scars are the ways we carry in our bodies the death of Jesus. I don't know what scars Paul might have been able to display, but he had been stoned, he had been beaten. and he had been scourged. He had even been bitten by a snake! I would be surprised if he had no scars on his body.

Now, I don't have any physical scars from my afflictions or persecutions, or criticisms and faultfindings, but—and these are just as real—I have spiritual scars. And as I've said, we are raised up from being stricken down by the power of the resurrection; we are healed because we know we are not forsaken, and we are not crushed because we are enabled to endure our afflictions.

When we celebrate Communion, one of the things we are doing is remembering the body of Christ broken and the blood of Christ poured out: "As often as you eat this bread and drink the cup, you proclaim the Lord's death until he comes" (1 Corinthians 11:26). Not only do we have physical reminders of Jesus's death because of our afflictions and persecutions, but we have a ritual that remembers His death. We receive within us, symbolically through the bread and the cup, the broken body and the shed blood of Jesus Christ. It becomes part of us, at least spiritually. Therefore "we always carry in our bodies the death of Jesus," and we do it in order "that the life of Jesus may also be made visible in our bodies" (2 Corinthians 4:10).

All believers should want their lives to testify to the love of God in Christ Jesus our Lord. We want to manifest His Spirit, His way, and His teaching in our manner of life: "It is no longer I who live, but it is Christ who lives in me" (Galatians 2:20). Our beliefs can identify us with our Savior to such a degree that He lives in us and through us.

"Death is at work in us, but life in you" (2 Corinthians 4:12). Our self-denial, our surrender to the purposes of Christ, our identifying with Jesus, all help manifest the grace of God at work in the world or at least in our own lives. People can see by our witness the suffering we are willing to endure in order to reveal the mercies of God to the hearts and minds of others. We have this ministry (2 Corinthians 4:1 NIV)! But we must never forget that "we have this treasure" (v. 7)—the treasure of God's light shining in our hearts (4:6a)—and it gives us "the light of the knowledge of the glory of God in the face of Jesus Christ" (4:6b)

Reflections on Psalm 23. *You anoint my head with oil; my cup overflows* (v.5b). Jesus said, "I am the gate of the sheep ... Whoever enters by me will be saved, and will come in and go out and find pasture" (John 10:7, 9). At the end of the day, the shepherd leads the flock back to the fold, where they are safe. But he becomes the gate himself. With his staff he allows one lamb at a time to come before him. He inspects them, removing any burrs that might irritate their skin, putting oil on any scratches they may have received, and bathing their faces with that salve. It is another sign of comfort for the sheep.

When we count our blessings, even in the midst of the threats that could strike us down, it revives us, and reminds us that our cups overflow!

SCRIPTURES

Here are some relevant passages of scripture to inspire a deeper understanding of "carrying the death of Jesus" from the biblical point of view.

"I am the resurrection and the life. Those who believe in me, even though they die, will live, and everyone who lives and believes in me will never die. (John 11:25–26)

Therefore we have been buried with him in baptism into death, so that, just as Christ was raised from the dead by the glory of the Father, so we too might walk in newness of life. For if we have been united with him in a death like his, we will certainly be united with him in a resurrection like his. (Romans 6:4–5)

Just as we have borne the image of the man of dust, we will also bear the image of the man of heaven. (1 Corinthians 15:49)

I have been crucified with Christ; and it is no longer I who live, but it is Christ who lives in me. And the life I now live in the flesh I live by faith in the Son of God, who loved me and gave himself for me. (Galatians 2:19b-20)

I want to know Christ and the power of his resurrection and the sharing of his sufferings by becoming like him in his death, if somehow I may attain the resurrection from the dead. (Philippians 3:10)

The saying is sure: If we have died with him, we will also live with him; if we endure, we will also reign with him. (2 Timothy 2:11–12)

WHAT TO DO

- > Manifest the death of Christ in your witness, in your testimony, and in your actions. Be sacrificial for the sake of others.
- > Deny yourself. A mother foregoes her own comfort when she delivers a new life into the world. A father works not just for himself but for the sake of his wife and children. The denials don't seem equal (by far!), but sacrificing our comforts identifies us with the sacrifice of Christ, though not equal.

> Think about what it could mean to be "crucified with Christ" (Galatians 2:19b).

> Think about what it could mean to be "united with him in a death like his" (Romans 6:5).

> Think about how people might seem to participate in "this present darkness" (Ephesians 6:12). What does "darkness" mean here?

> Think about how your cup overflows (Psalm 23:5b). Does it overflow for your own sake or for the sake of others?

PRAYER

Almighty God, my belief in Jesus is my resurrection and my life, but I know I must also die with Him to receive this promise. Help me to know Christ so well that I can truly share in His sufferings, that I may truly be crucified with Him, and that I may find new life in the power of His resurrection. I ask this prayer in Jesus's name. Amen.

POEM
To My Future

You are waiting; you are free.
You're an inside part of me.
You're a question; you're a dream.
You are starlight on a beam.

I have heard a soft command
Like a warm, compelling hand,
Like a distant sounding call—
But are you really there at all?

There's a song we can't set free
Until there is a melody.
There's an onward-looking eye
That sees beyond our farthest cry.

You're so close, but far away,
And when you come, I hope you'll stay.

CHAPTER 8

We Have the Same Spirit of God

But just as we have the same spirit of God
that is in accordance with scripture—
"I believed and so I spoke"—
we also believe, and so we speak,
because we know
that the one who raised the Lord Jesus
will raise us also with Jesus,
and will bring us with you into his presence.
Yes, everything is for your sake,
so that grace, as it extends to more and more people,
may increase thanksgiving, to the glory of God.
1 Corinthians 4:13–15

We have the Holy Spirit. By the grace of God at work in our lives, we have the Spirit of Christ. *This* is "the light of the knowledge of the glory of God" (2 Corinthians 4:6). This is the treasure in the clay jars of our lives. This is what gives us confidence; it makes us bold and helps us proclaim the gospel. It gives us peace; it gives us wisdom. And "if any of you is lacking in wisdom, ask God, who gives to all generously and ungrudgingly, and it will be given to you" (James 1:5).

Imagine the possibility of having a superpower and not knowing it. Some of the depictions of Superman's younger years as Superboy show how he learned over time what he could do. He didn't know he had super hearing until one day he overheard some conversations that helped him know when to step in and defend another boy. He didn't know he had super vision until he saw in the distance something about to happen that would have injured some friends—and as he hurried to the scene to rescue them, he discovered also that he had super speed. It goes on like that until he realizes he has many superpowers and is invulnerable in many ways.

Well, in the same way, we are very vulnerable until we discover that we have the "superpower" we need to endure our afflictions and persecutions. But we don't discover this ability until we face those trials in our lives. Meanwhile, the grace in our lives, "as it extends to more and more people, may increase thanksgiving, to the glory of God" (2 Corinthians 4:15). And "whatever you do, do everything for the glory of God" (1 Corinthians 10:31).

One Sunday in one of the churches I served, during the formal time of greeting that was always a part of the worship services I led, a young man came forward to shake my hand. I didn't recognize him at first, though I thought I knew him. As he greeted me, he asked me if I knew who he was. I couldn't quite make a connection until after he told me his name. Then I realized why he looked familiar. I *had* known him, and now I recognized him as a former member at an earlier church. What a treat.

After worship, we invited him over to the parsonage for lunch. We talked for several hours. One of the things he shared was an exercise in a sociology class in college. The professor had guided the students with the question, "Who were the most influential people in your life as you were going through your teen years?" This young man had said that I was second, after his mom!

Wow! I had not known until then. I never knew whether I had been a positive influence in his life or what had happened to him. He was just one of the many teens in the congregation's youth fellowship. I was at that church for only four years. It was a difficult congregation in many ways, but they grew in numbers, in financial health, and in spirit, though they could have gone a lot further. As it was, they never really grew to achieve what I believed they had the potential to accomplish and are now a part-time appointment. But ten years after I left, this young man had made the challenges in that congregation well worth it to me. I felt as if I had fulfilled my purpose for him if not for others at that church. Not long after that, I learned that I was spoken well of by many there. That filled my heart. And it does so again as I remember it.

My cousin's wife recently retired from teaching. One of the things she said in reflecting on her forty–year career was that her father, a pastor, had told her, "Never underestimate the value of planting seeds!" The ministry is often a matter of planting seeds. Sometimes those seeds are germinating in our own lives. Something grows within us, and it is often when we need it most that there are fruits to prove the value of planting seeds. And often there are fruits that appear in the lives of others, long after we have shared in ministry together.

Something is always happening that makes it all worthwhile. And the reward is that "as it extends to more and more people, [it] may increase thanksgiving" (2 Corinthians 4:15).

Reflections on Psalm 23. *Surely goodness and mercy shall follow me all the days of my life.* (v. 6a) We leave a trail! Sometimes it may be hard to distinguish, but someone, hopefully many, will know we've been there. We offered our leadership as sheepdogs, and we endured!

SCRIPTURES

Here are some relevant passages of scripture to inspire a deeper understanding of what it means from the biblical point of view to claim that "we have the same Spirit of God."

I will pour out my spirit on all flesh; your sons and your daughters shall prophesy, your old men shall dream dreams, and your young men shall see visions. Even on the male and female slaves, in those days, I will pour out my spirit. (Joel 2:28–29)

"I baptize you with water; but one who is more powerful than I is coming; I am not worthy to untie the thong of his sandals. He will baptize you with the Holy Spirit and fire." (John the Baptist Luke 3:16)

"And see, I am sending upon you what my Father promised, so stay here in the city until you have been clothed with power from on high." (Luke 24:49)

"I will ask the Father, and he will give you another Advocate, to be with you forever. This is the Spirit of truth, whom the world cannot receive, because it neither sees him nor knows him. You know him, because he abides with you, and he will be in you." (John 14:16–17)

"But the Advocate, the Holy Spirit, whom the Father will send in my name, will teach you everything, and remind you of all that I have said to you." (John 14:26)

When the Advocate comes, whom I will send from the Father, the Spirit of truth who comes from the Father, he will testify on my behalf. (John 15:26)

"When the Spirit of truth comes, he will guide you into all the truth." (John 16:13)

"You will receive power when the Holy Spirit has come upon you; and you will be my witnesses in Jerusalem, in all Judea and Samaria, and to the ends of the earth." (Acts 1:8)

Peter said to them, "Repent, and be baptized every one of you in the name of Jesus Christ so that your sins may be forgiven, and you will receive the gift of the Holy Spirit." (Acts 2:38)

But you are not in the flesh; you are in the Spirit, since the Spirit of God dwells in you. Anyone who does not have the Spirit of Christ does not belong to him. (Romans 8:9)

Do you not know that your body is a temple of the Holy Spirit within you, which you have from God, and that you are not your own. (1 Corinthians 6:19)

God did not give us a spirit of cowardice, but rather a spirit of power and of love, and of self-discipline. (2 Timothy 1:7)

What to Do

- ▸ Plant seeds!
- ▸ Learn this old Greek proverb: "Blessed are those who plant trees under whose shade they will never sit." What does that mean to you?
- ▸ Consider how the Advocate can work. How has the Advocate worked in your life?
- ▸ Consider the idea of being baptized with fire. What does it mean?
- ▸ Consider how Paul has said that grace "extends to more and more people." How is grace extending to people through your witness?

Prayer

O God, by Your grace Your Spirit dwells within me. And though there may be times when I may feel afflicted, perplexed, persecuted, and struck down, I know that I will never be crushed, driven to despair, forsaken, or destroyed, for You have the last word in my life. May that word be peace. I ask this prayer in Jesus's name. Amen.

POEM
A Rainbow Day

Once I saw a rainbow day
With simple streams of light at bay.
And angels sang from heaven above,
And there was life, and there was love.

I saw a meadow, and I saw peace.
I saw a fawn alone, at ease.
I saw a garden along the way.
O Lord, I saw a rainbow day!

Once I saw a dove on wing
Sailing round to make a ring,
And after it circled heaven above,
I had dreams, and they were love.

I heard stories dreamers told;
I saw good, and I saw gold.
I saw a promise along the way
O Lord, I saw a rainbow day!

A Final Promise

So we do not lose heart.
Even though our outer nature is wasting away,
our inner nature is being renewed every day.
For this slight momentary affliction
is preparing for us an eternal weight of glory
beyond all measure,
because we look not at what can be seen,
for what can be seen is temporary, but we look to what is eternal.
2 Corinthians 4:16–18

God bless us all!

A final reflection from Psalm 23. Surely goodness and mercy shall follow me all the days of my life, and *I shall dwell in the house of the Lord my whole life long.* (v. 6) Our focus is future-oriented. "We look to what is eternal" (2 Corinthians 4:18).

POEM
Morning of Hope

Of raging old and beaten hearts
I've seen so many stops and starts,
But never have my dreams been drawn
To wish so much to carry on.

Hold on now and let peace flow.
Pray with me and let love grow.
There's so much left for us to see,
And I would like you there with me
When all the stars begin to shine
So I can call them yours and mine.
"Ours," I'd say, and we could stay
In harmony and truly pray.

If I should never hope again,
This morning starts beginning's end.

Printed in the United States
by Baker & Taylor Publisher Services